EZ JAZZ

*Seven Easy-to-Play
Jazz Piano Solos For Any Age*

by

Bert Konowitz

© Copyright 2003 by LEE ROBERTS MUSIC PUBLICATIONS, Inc.
International Copyright Secured
ALL RIGHTS RESERVED
Unauthorized copying, arranging, adapting, recording or
public performance is an infringement of copyright.
Infringers are liable under the law.

BLUE NOTE BOOGIE

BERT KONOWITZ

CHOO-CHOO STOMP

BERT KONOWITZ

JAZZ SPOOKS

BERT KONOWITZ

JAZZ WALTZ

BERT KONOWITZ

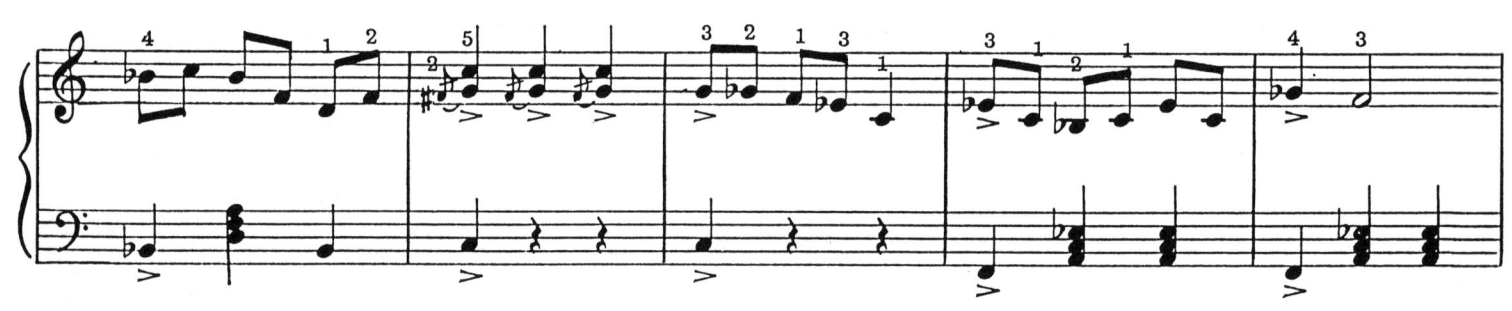

LAZY DAZE

BERT KONOWITZ

Raga Rock

BERT KONOWITZ

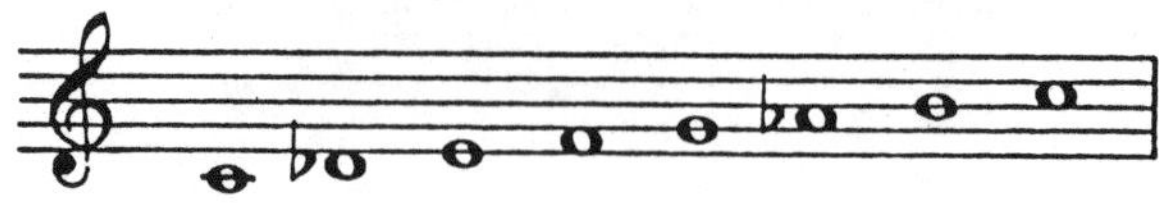

The raga Bhairava, a Hindu "mode" or "scale"

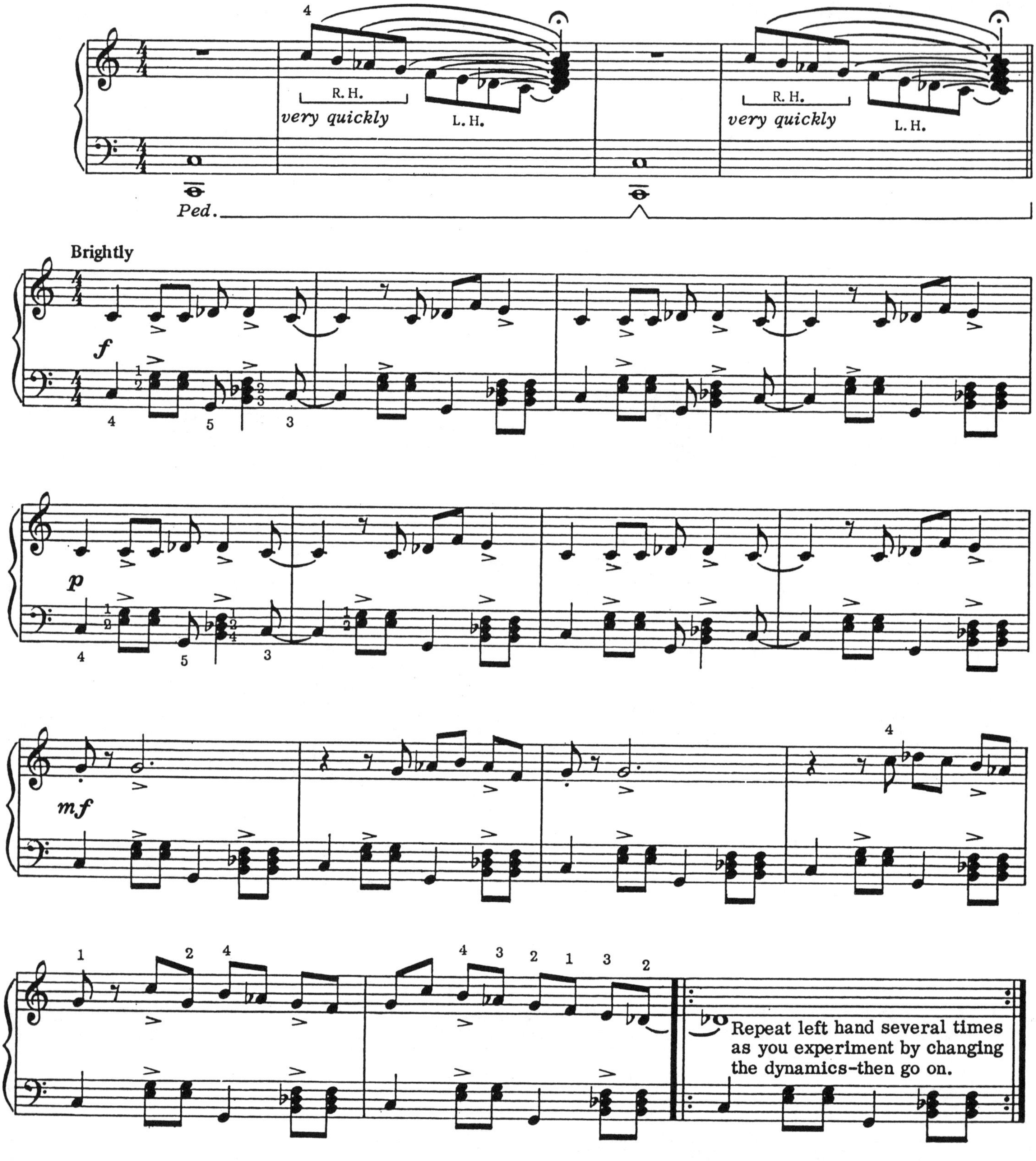
R. H.
very quickly
L. H.
Ped.
Brightly
Repeat left hand several times as you experiment by changing the dynamics–then go on.

POUNDIN' THE BEAT

BERT KONOWITZ